Life Under the Sea
Clownfish

by Cari Meister

Ideas for Parents and Teachers

Bullfrog Books let children practice reading informational text at the earliest reading levels. Repetition, familiar words, and photo labels support early readers.

Before Reading

- Ask the child to think about clownfish. Ask: What do you know about clownfish?
- Look at the picture glossary together. Read and discuss the words.

Read the Book

- "Walk" through the book and look at the photos. Let the child ask questions. Point out the photo labels.
- Read the book to the child, or have him or her read independently.

After Reading

- Prompt the child to think more. Ask: What do you think a clownfish feels like? What would it be like to live in an anemone?

Bullfrog Books are published by Jump!
5357 Penn Avenue South
Minneapolis, MN 55419
www.jumplibrary.com

Copyright © 2014 Jump! International copyright reserved in all countries. No part of this book may be reproduced in any form without written permission from the publisher.

Library of Congress Cataloging-in-
Meister, Cari.
 Clownfish / by Cari Meister.
   p. cm. -- (Bullfrog books. Life under the sea)
 Summary: "This photo-illustrated book for early readers tells the story of clownfish making a nest and protecting their eggs"-- Provided by publisher.
 Audience: K to grade 3.
 Includes bibliographical references and index.
 ISBN 978-1-62031-030-4 (hardcover : alk. paper) --
ISBN 978-1-62496-048-2 (ebook)
 1. Anemonefishes--Juvenile literature.
 2. Anemonefishes--Behavior--Juvenile literature. I. Title.
 QL638.P77M45 2014
 597'.72--dc23   2013001955

Series Editor   Rebecca Glaser
Book Designer   Ellen Huber
Photo Researcher   Heather Dreisbach

Photo Credits: Alamy, 20–21, 23ml; Bigstock, 4, 14; Corbis, 3, 9, 12–13, 18, 23bl, 24; Dreamstime, 6–7, 8, 22; Shutterstock, cover, 1, 5, 10–11, 15, 16, 19, 23tl, 23tr, 23mr, 23br; SuperStock, 17

Printed in the United States of America at Corporate Graphics, North Mankato, Minnesota.
5-2013 / PO 1003

10 9 8 7 6 5 4 3 2 1

Table of Contents

Looking for a Nest

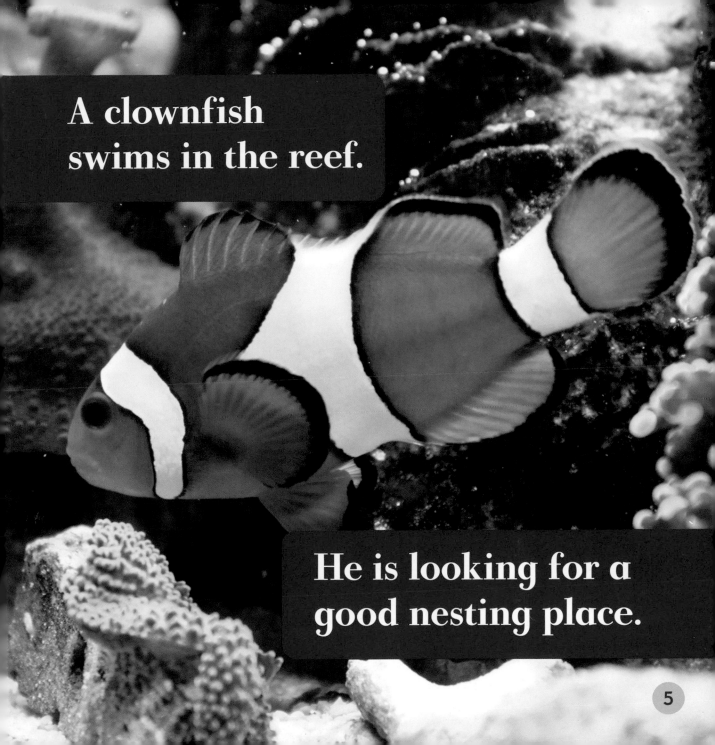

A clownfish swims in the reef.

He is looking for a good nesting place.

5

Look!
A flat rock.

It is perfect.

Now he
is ready.

The clownfish swims home.

He lives in an anemone.

Anemones use poison to sting fish to eat.

anemone

Clownfish do not get stung.

They have special
slime on their scales.

It protects them.

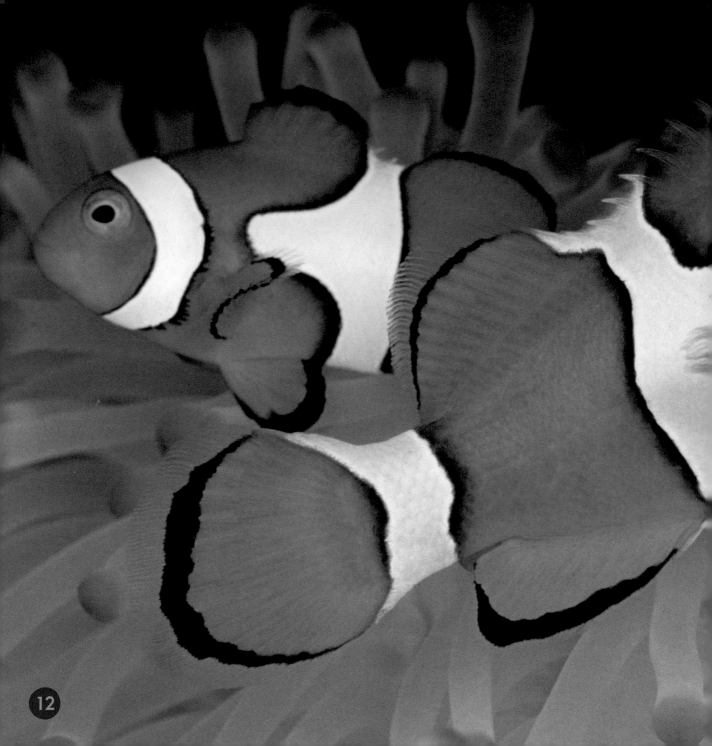

The clownfish
finds his mate.

He chases her.
He bites.

He touches her with his fin.

Follow me to the nest!

The female drops
hundreds of eggs.

Then she swims home.

The male guards the nest.

Oh no! A fish!
He wants to eat the eggs.

The clownfish
chases him away.

Hooray!

The eggs
are safe!

Parts of a Clownfish

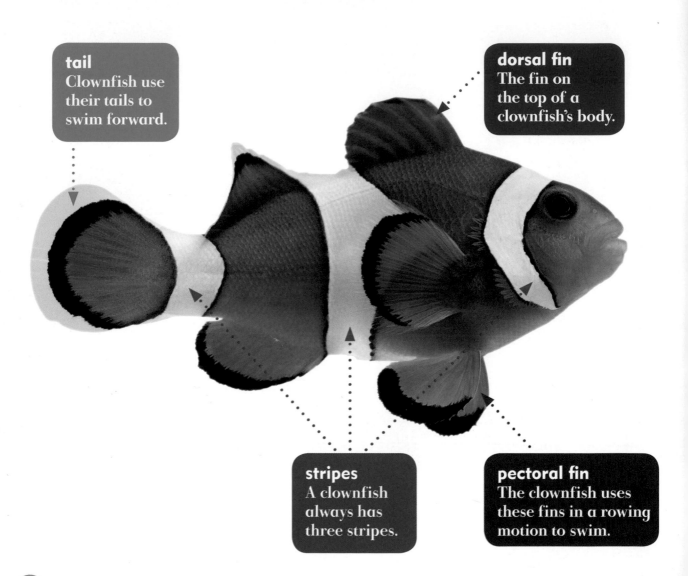

tail
Clownfish use their tails to swim forward.

dorsal fin
The fin on the top of a clownfish's body.

stripes
A clownfish always has three stripes.

pectoral fin
The clownfish uses these fins in a rowing motion to swim.

Picture Glossary

anemone
A type of sea animal with long, stinging tentacles.

poison
A substance that kills or injures living things.

mate
A fish's partner; a clownfish needs a mate to make babies.

reef
A ridge of rocks, sand, or coral that comes up near a water's surface.

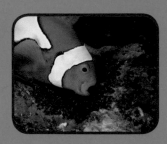

nest
A place where eggs are placed before they've hatched.

scales
Hard plates that cover fish.

Index

To Learn More

Learning more is as easy as 1, 2, 3.

1) Go to www.factsurfer.com

2) Enter "clownfish" into the search box.

3) Click the "Surf" button to see a list of websites.

With factsurfer.com, finding more information is just a click away.